MENTAL
Arithmetic

EDUCATIONAL

CONTENTS

INTRODUCTION

Welcome to your *Mental Arithmetic Skills* booklet

It is designed to help you to practise your maths skills **in your head**. Please do not use a calculator!

In Year 9, you have to take your Key Stage 3 National Tests (often called SATs) in Mathematics. This booklet is designed to help you to prepare for the tests, especially the Mental Arithmetic Higher Test (covering National Curriculum Levels 4 up to 7). In the test, you listen to a cassette tape of questions and write down your answers. You get only a limited amount of time for each question, so it is important that you improve your speed of calculation -while still getting the answer right, of course!

The best way to use this booklet is to get someone to read out the questions to you, going across the page. Ask your parents, your friends or your teacher to do this. You could also test yourself by making sure you cover up the answers on the right-hand side and doing maybe four questions at a time.

The key to improvement is to **keep practising over and over again** until you are confident.

Each set of questions becomes more difficult as you work through it. There are also tips and examples to help you. **You should go through these before attempting each set of questions.**

At the end of the booklet, there are two typical SATs papers, each with an answer sheet that you fill in while someone reads you the questions. Work through the tests under timed conditions as suggested.

We all need to improve our mental arithmetic and imagery, so I hope this booklet will prove to be an invaluable aid for **everyone, not just those taking the SATs!**

SHORT Multiplication

You should know your times tables well enough to answer these correctly. They are the basis for so much arithmetic and really boost your confidence if you know them well.

TOP*tips*

It doesn't matter which way round you multiply two numbers together.

If either number is even, their **product** is also even, so...

if both numbers are odd, their **product** must also be odd.

Work out these in your head.

3×4	4×2	4×4	7×2	12, 8, 16, 14
3×3	6×4	4×6	6×3	9, 24, 24, 18

TOP*tips*

Multiples of **5** always end in either **5** or **0**.

2×5	6×5	5×8	5×5	10, 30, 40, 25

Multiples of **6** are multiples of both **2** and **3** (and are **always even**).

2×6	5×6	4×6	6×6	12, 30, 24, 36

Multiples of **8** are multiples of both **2** and **4** (and are **always even**).

3×8	5×8	8×6	7×8	24, 40, 48, 56

If you **add** together the **two digits** of the multiples of **9**, you always get **9**.

4×9	9×6	3×9	5×9	36, 54, 27, 45

Now practise these over and over until you get them all right!

3×7	5×4	6×5	7×4	21, 20, 30, 28
5×7	6×6	8×4	3×9	35, 36, 32, 27
8×5	4×9	6×8	7×7	40, 36, 48, 49
9×6	8×7	5×9	8×6	54, 56, 45, 48

				Answers
5 × 6	2 × 7	6 × 8	4 × 4	30, 14, 48, 16
6 × 7	8 × 3	9 × 9	2 × 6	42, 24, 81, 12
8 × 8	4 × 5	6 × 9	7 × 4	64, 20, 54, 28
9 × 7	5 × 3	8 × 9	7 × 6	63, 15, 72, 42
2 × 8	9 × 6	7 × 3	8 × 5	16, 54, 21, 40
5 × 5	7 × 8	9 × 5	9 × 3	25, 56, 45, 27
4 × 3	8 × 6	6 × 4	2 × 9	12, 48, 24, 18
6 × 6	7 × 7	8 × 8	9 × 9	36, 49, 64, 81

MORE Multiplication
(product less than 100)

To multiply by 13, times by 10, then times by 3 and add: e.g. 13 × 6 is the same as **10 × 6** plus **3 × 6** which is 60 + 18 = **78**

Work out these in your head.

12 × 7	11 × 5	6 × 14	8 × 12	84, 55, 84, 96
13 × 5	9 × 11	13 × 4	12 × 6	65, 99, 52, 72
7 × 14	15 × 6	7 × 11	14 × 4	98, 90, 77, 56
14 × 5	16 × 4	3 × 17	4 × 19	70, 64, 51, 76
5 × 17	18 × 3	6 × 16	7 × 13	85, 54, 96, 91

EVEN MORE Multiplication
(product greater than 100)

To multiply by 27, times by 20, then times by 7 and add: e.g. 27 × 7 is the same as **20 × 7** plus **7 × 7** which is 140 + 49 = **189**

Work out these in your head.

23 × 5	19 × 6	3 × 42	21 × 8	115, 114, 126, 168
6 × 27	4 × 31	17 × 7	5 × 22	162, 124, 119, 110
21 × 9	56 × 3	5 × 37	28 × 6	189, 168, 185, 168
7 × 23	26 × 8	34 × 5	4 × 44	161, 208, 170, 176

LONG **Multiplication**

Split long multiplication into simple stages:

e.g. 16×11 is the same as $16 \times$ **10** plus 16 which is

$160 + 16 =$ **176**

13×12 is the same as $13 \times$ **10** plus $13 \times$ **2** which is

$130 + 26 =$ **156**

14×18 is the same as $14 \times$ **20** subtract $14 \times$ **2** which

is $280 - 28 =$ **252**

23×19 is the same as $23 \times$ **20** subtract 23 which is

$460 - 23 =$ **437**

Work out these in your head.

14×11	16×12	11×17	154, 192, 187
14×12	19×12	22×11	168, 228, 242
16×19	13×21	17×12	304, 273, 204
15×14	25×16	13×19	210, 400, 247
18×22	15×29	23×12	396, 435, 276
16×21	21×17	31×13	336, 357, 403

To multiply by **25**, first **times** by **100** then **divide** by **4**:

e.g. 16×25 is the same as $16 \times$ **100 divided** by **4**

which is $1600 \div 4 =$ **400**

To multiply by **15** first **times** by **30** then **divide** by **2**:

e.g. 17×15 is the same as $17 \times$ **30 divided** by **2** which

is $510 \div 2 =$ **255**

Work out these in your head.

12×29	15×25	11×42	348, 375, 462
36×21	50×28	31×32	756, 1400, 992
25×36	22×18	41×17	900, 396, 697
32×22	51×16	21×69	704, 816, 1449
44×35	63×98		1540, 6174

SHORT Division

Dividing is the reverse of multiplying – easy if you know your times tables!

Work out these in your head.

Answers

9 ÷ 3	6 ÷ 2	8 ÷ 4	10 ÷ 2	3, 3, 2, 5
14 ÷ 2	18 ÷ 3	15 ÷ 5	16 ÷ 4	7, 6, 3, 4
21 ÷ 3	24 ÷ 8	12 ÷ 6	18 ÷ 9	7, 3, 2, 2
12 ÷ 3	28 ÷ 4	27 ÷ 3	32 ÷ 8	4, 7, 9, 4
35 ÷ 5	36 ÷ 9	32 ÷ 4	28 ÷ 7	7, 4, 8, 4
36 ÷ 6	40 ÷ 8	49 ÷ 7	48 ÷ 6	6, 5, 7, 8
56 ÷ 8	42 ÷ 7	54 ÷ 6	63 ÷ 9	7, 6, 9, 7
72 ÷ 9	48 ÷ 8	81 ÷ 9	64 ÷ 8	8, 6, 9, 8

In the next group of questions, you will **divide through each digit** as you go:
e.g. 408 ÷ 4   Work out **4 ÷ 4**, then **0 ÷ 4**, then **8 ÷ 4**, to get the answer **102**.

Work out these in your head.

63 ÷ 3	48 ÷ 2	88 ÷ 4	96 ÷ 3	21, 24, 22, 32
62 ÷ 2	39 ÷ 3	90 ÷ 3	86 ÷ 2	31, 13, 30, 43
84 ÷ 4	46 ÷ 2	66 ÷ 3	48 ÷ 4	21, 23, 22, 12
264 ÷ 2	690 ÷ 3	428 ÷ 2	9396 ÷ 3	132, 230, 214, 3132

In the next group of questions, the first digit is **too small** to divide into. So, you will need to start with the **first two digits**, then divide through as above.

Work out these in your head.

124 ÷ 4	159 ÷ 3	246 ÷ 6	210 ÷ 7	31, 53, 41, 30
189 ÷ 9	168 ÷ 4	255 ÷ 5	328 ÷ 8	21, 42, 51, 41
186 ÷ 3	264 ÷ 2	426 ÷ 6	567 ÷ 7	62, 132, 71, 81
360 ÷ 9	728 ÷ 8	306 ÷ 6	3550 ÷ 5	40, 91, 51, 710

In the next group of questions, you will need to carry the remainders as you go:
e.g. 54 ÷ 3. First work out
   5 ÷ 3, which is **1** remainder **2**. Then work out
   24 ÷ 3, which is **8**. So, the answer is **18**.

Work out these in your head.

42 ÷ 3	78 ÷ 6	85 ÷ 5	57 ÷ 3	96 ÷ 4	14, 13, 17, 19, 24
91 ÷ 7	72 ÷ 4	81 ÷ 3	72 ÷ 3	90 ÷ 5	13, 18, 27, 24, 18
84 ÷ 6	96 ÷ 8	108 ÷ 4	177 ÷ 3	216 ÷ 9	14, 12, 27, 59, 24
336 ÷ 7					48

ADDING Whole Numbers

How quickly can you add up each list of numbers?
Under 10 seconds per list is superb.

Answers

A	B	C	D	E	F	G	H
4	2	8	7	3	5	9	6
7	4	3	2	5	6	2	2
5	6	4	5	7	2	5	7
8	2	9	2	1	8	3	1
2	9	6	9	8	6	7	9
7	8	8	5	3	4	5	6
5	4	2	7	9	3	8	8
9	6	9	4	9	9	8	7
2	7	5	8	4	7	1	7
5	7	6	6	7	8	5	4
7	4	2	8	5	3	9	9
4	9	3	1	6	8	6	1
9	1	7	7	6	6	4	3
7	4	4	4	1	1	4	5
3	7	6	7	2	5	7	4
2	6	1	5	7	6	5	7
6	4	7	2	8	2	9	6
5	8	4	5	4	7	2	5

A 97

B 98

C 94

D 94

E 95

F 96

G 99

H 97

Check by going back upwards through each list.

TOP*tips*

When adding numbers of two or more digits, you must think in units, tens, hundreds, etc. So remember to keep track of what you are carrying.

Work out these in your head.

13 + 36	17 + 25	43 + 37	55 + 26	49, 42, 80, 81
15 + 28	43 + 35	29 + 52	46 + 28	43, 78, 81, 74
31 + 47	85 + 18	66 + 26	27 + 75	78, 103, 92, 102
61 + 72	72 + 49	83 + 36	47 + 78	133, 121, 119, 125
126 + 43	407 + 69	618 + 71	265 + 29	169, 476, 689, 294
335 + 27	713 + 68	847 + 45	557 + 44	362, 781, 892, 601
472 + 64	253 + 82	766 + 53	576 + 47	536, 335, 819, 623
338 + 87	289 + 68	576 + 67	878 + 88	425, 357, 643, 966
135 + 123	242 + 334	463 + 516	248 + 134	258, 576, 979, 382
358 + 427	624 + 267	482 + 335	646 + 274	785, 891, 817, 920
857 + 368				1225

SUBTRACTING Whole Numbers

Work out these in your head.

16 − 3	19 − 5	12 − 3	15 − 7		13, 14, 9, 8
11 − 6	20 − 9	23 − 4	24 − 6		5, 11, 19, 18
16 − 7	14 − 8	22 − 7	33 − 6		9, 6, 15, 27
31 − 9	40 − 8	54 − 7	62 − 9		22, 32, 47, 53

Getting harder.

38 − 13	25 − 14	49 − 23	77 − 41	25, 11, 26, 36
56 − 35	85 − 32	69 − 54	98 − 72	21, 53, 15, 26
136 − 24	185 − 41	259 − 26	287 − 142	112, 144, 233, 145
399 − 223	475 − 211	568 − 317		176, 264, 251

To subtract numbers ending in **9**, **add 1 to both the numbers**, then do the subtraction:
e.g. 76 − 29 is the same as doing **77 − 30** which gives the answer **47**.

Work out these in your head.

37 − 19	46 − 19	53 − 19	48 − 29	18, 27, 34, 19
84 − 29	91 − 29	67 − 39	92 − 39	55, 62, 28, 53
110 − 49	143 − 29	175 − 59	298 − 59	61, 114, 116, 239
376 − 159	544 − 219	861 − 329		217, 325, 532

Add to both numbers before you subtract:
e.g. 64 − 28 is the same as doing **66 − 30** (adding 2 to both numbers), which gives you the answer **36**.

Work out these in your head.

35 − 18	57 − 18	86 − 28	72 − 17	17, 39, 58, 55
41 − 12	64 − 17	74 − 16	91 − 28	29, 47, 58, 63
85 − 38	97 − 49	63 − 16	71 − 47	47, 48, 47, 24
162 − 48	281 − 134	553 − 337	112 − 37	114, 147, 216, 75
246 − 89	425 − 147			157, 278

MULTIPLYING **by 10, 100, 1000**

When multiplying a **whole number by 10**, **100** or **1000**, put **one**, **two**, or **three noughts** respectively on the **end** of the number:

e.g. $35 \times 10 = 350$ $47 \times 100 = 4700$
$11 \times 1000 = 11\,000$

Work out these in your head

13×10	21×10	15×10
24×100	15×1000	52×10
98×10	103×100	40×1000

130, 210, 150
2400, 15 000, 520
980, 10 300, 40 000

To multiply by **20**, first **times by 2** and then put a **nought on the end**:
e.g. $13 \times 20 = 260$

To multiply by **300**, first **times by 3** and then put **two noughts on the end**:
e.g. $7 \times 300 = 2100$

Work out these in your head

4×20	6×20	3×30	5×30
3×40	7×20	8×40	6×50
60×3	70×4	5×90	80×8
4×200	300×7	5×5000	

80, 120, 90, 150
120, 140, 320, 300
180, 280, 450, 640
800, 2100, 25 000

11×50	12×30	16×20
20×25	34×20	40×30
60×90	50×80	15×400
60×700	43×2000	18×300
31×40	52×500	

550, 360, 320
500, 680, 1200
5400, 4000, 6000
42 000, 86 000, 5400
1240, 26 000

To multiply a **decimal by 10**, **move** the decimal point **one place to the right**:
e.g. $4.32 \times 10 = 43.2$ $0.567 \times 10 = 5.67$
$30.8 \times 10 = 308$

Work out these in your head

3.41×10	4.65×10	5.27×10
11.63×10	59.49×10	40.02×10
6.2×10	3.9×10	7.6×10
25.4×10	67.8×10	50.9×10
0.235×10	10×0.061	7.018×10
0.401×10	10×3.007	65.904×10

34.1, 46.5, 52.7
116.3, 594.9, 400.2
62, 39, 76
254, 678, 509
2.35, 0.61, 70.18
4.01, 30.07, 659.04

To multiply a **decimal by 100, move** the decimal point **two places to the right**:

e.g. $3.843 \times 100 = 384.3$ $6.21 \times 100 = 621$

$7.5 \times 100 = 750$

Work out these in your head

		Answers
5.642×100	86.265×100	564.2, 8626.5
70.314×100	6.39×100	7031.4, 639,
4.46×100	13.82×100	446, 1382
5.7×100	27.9×100	570, 2790
60.5×100	0.14×100	6050, 14
0.08×100	0.006×100	8, 0.6
100×0.6	0.75×100	60, 75
100×1.2	0.9×100	120, 90
100×1.01	9.09×100	101, 909
0.2×1000	6.08×1000	200, 6080
4.725×1000		4725

DIVIDING **by 10, 100, 1000**

When dividing a **whole number** which **ends in noughts by 10**, **100**, or **1000**, knock off **one**, **two** or **three noughts** respectively from the **end** of the number:

e.g. $460 \div 10 = 46$ $3800 \div 100 = 38$

$17\,000 \div 1000 = 17$

Work out these in your head

			Answers
$250 \div 10$	$120 \div 10$	$1970 \div 10$	25, 12, 197
$80 \div 10$	$200 \div 10$	$3500 \div 10$	8, 20, 350
$300 \div 100$	$1400 \div 100$	$7000 \div 100$	3, 14, 70
$2000 \div 100$	$8000 \div 1000$	$10\,000 \div 1000$	20, 8, 10

To divide by **20**, knock off **one nought** and **divide by 2**:

e.g. $240 \div 20 = 12$

To divide by **300**, knock off **two noughts** and **divide by 3**:

e.g. $2700 \div 300 = 9$

Work out these in your head

160 ÷ 20	120 ÷ 20	280 ÷ 20	320 ÷ 20
460 ÷ 20	500 ÷ 20	150 ÷ 30	270 ÷ 30
2000 ÷ 40	180 ÷ 60	360 ÷ 90	3000 ÷ 50
2400 ÷ 300	1800 ÷ 200	4000 ÷ 500	3600 ÷ 600
36 000 ÷ 2000		64 000 ÷ 4000	

Answers

8, 6, 14, 16
23, 25, 5, 9
50, 3, 4, 60
8, 9, 8, 6
18, 16

When there are **no noughts**, or **not enough noughts**, on the end of a number, you have to move the **decimal point**. To divide by 10, **move** the decimal point **one place to the left**.

e.g. 25 ÷ 10 = 2.5   13.6 ÷ 10 = 1.36
     2.98 ÷ 10 = 0.298

Work out these in your head

36 ÷ 10	22 ÷ 10	51 ÷ 10	17 ÷ 10
5 ÷ 10	8 ÷ 10	1 ÷ 10	4 ÷ 10
11 ÷ 10	12.5 ÷ 10	25.7 ÷ 10	38.4 ÷ 10
4.6 ÷ 10	7.5 ÷ 10	2.9 ÷ 10	
60.3 ÷ 10	5.78 ÷ 10	9.01 ÷ 10	

3.6, 2.2, 5.1, 1.7
0.5, 0.8, 0.1, 0.4
1.1, 1.25, 2.57, 3.84
0.46, 0.75, 0.29
6.03, 0.578, 0.901

To divide by **100**, **move** the decimal point **two places to the left**:

e.g. 34 ÷ 100 = 0.34   12.8 ÷ 100 = 0.128
     4.6 ÷ 100 = 0.046

Work out these in your head

12 ÷ 100	29 ÷ 100	57 ÷ 100
86 ÷ 100	134 ÷ 100	291 ÷ 100
449 ÷ 100	803 ÷ 100	2375 ÷ 100
14.5 ÷ 100	29.3 ÷ 100	78.2 ÷ 100
136.7 ÷ 100	558.4 ÷ 100	962.2 ÷ 100
3.9 ÷ 100	7.4 ÷ 100	6.08 ÷ 100

0.12, 0.29, 0.57
0.86, 1.34, 2.91
4.49, 8.03, 23.75
0.145, 0.293, 0.782
1.367, 5.584, 9.622
0.039, 0.074,
0.0608

MULTIPLYING AND DIVIDING
Decimals

When **multiplying** by a decimal, first do the calculation **ignoring the decimal point**. Then **insert it in the correct place** in your answer:

e.g. 8×0.2 First, work out $8 \times 2 = 16$, then insert the decimal point: 1.6

6×0.03 First, work out $6 \times 3 = 18$, then insert the decimal point: 0.18

Work out these in your head.

4×0.4	5×0.3	7×0.7	6×0.5	1.6, 1.5, 4.9, 3
12×0.3	15×0.1	57×0.1	20×0.6	3.6, 1.5, 5.7, 12
50×0.8	100×0.75	400×0.7	0.3×600	40, 75, 280, 180
800×0.15				120

6×0.02	3×0.05	8×0.04	0.12, 0.15, 0.32
11×0.06	17×0.01	44×0.01	0.66, 0.17, 0.44
30×0.03	40×0.06	0.07×50	0.9, 2.4, 3.5
700×0.02	0.08×600	3000×0.09	14, 48, 270

When **dividing** by a decimal, first do the calculation **ignoring the decimal point**. Then **insert it in the correct place** in your answer.

e.g. $80 \div 0.2 = 400$ since $80 \div 20 = 4$
$$80 \div 2 = 40$$
$$80 \div 0.2 = 400$$
$$80 \div 0.02 = 4000$$

TOP*tips*
The smaller the number you're dividing by, the bigger the answer.

Work out these in your head.

$1.6 \div 0.8$	$3.6 \div 0.6$	$4.5 \div 0.5$	$4 \div 0.2$	2, 6, 9, 20
$9 \div 0.3$	$12 \div 0.4$	$32 \div 0.8$	$45 \div 0.9$	30, 30, 40, 50
$88 \div 1.1$	$150 \div 0.3$	$100 \div 0.1$	$420 \div 0.6$	80, 500, 1000, 700
$375 \div 0.1$	$560 \div 0.2$	$600 \div 0.15$		3750, 2800, 4000

13

$1.4 \div 0.07$	$2.4 \div 0.06$	$3.5 \div 0.05$	$6 \div 0.02$
$8 + 0.04$	$21 \div 0.03$	$42 \div 0.07$	$60 \div 0.06$
$81 \div 0.09$	$100 \div 0.01$		
$147 \div 0.01$	$650 \div 0.05$		

NEGATIVE Numbers

–10 –9 –8 –7 –6 –5 –4 –3 –2 –1 0 1 2 3 4 5 6 7 8 9 10

← – negative direction | positive direction + →

Numbers can be represented by points on a straight line, called the number line. Those to the left of zero are **negative numbers**. They occur when you subtract a big number from a small number:

e.g. $5 - 11 = -6$ Start at 5 and count 11 steps to the left.

TOP*tips*
Notice that $11 - 5 = 6$

Work out these in your head

$4 - 7$	$2 - 6$	$1 - 3$	$6 - 7$	$-3, -4, -2, -1$
$5 - 12$	$3 - 14$	$8 - 30$	$16 - 21$	$-7, -11, -22, -5$
$0 - 9$	$-2 - 3$	$-5 - 4$	$-10 - 6$	$-9, -5, -9, -16$
$-15 - 15$	$-31 - 24$	$-49 - 36$		$-30, -55, -85$

You can add a negative number to another number: e.g.
$4 + -9 = -5$ This is just the same as doing $4 - 9 = -5$

Work out these in your head

$3 + -6$	$5 + -7$	$8 + -9$	$9 + -4$	$-3, -2, -1, 5$
$7 + -3$	$14 + -8$	$6 + -11$	$15 + -14$	$4, 6, -5, 1$
$-6 + -3$	$-2 + -5$	$-4 + -7$	$-12 + -9$	$-9, -7, -11, -21$

You can also subtract a negative number from another number: e.g. $6 - -4 = 10$ This is just the same as doing $6 + 4 = 10$

Work out these in your head

5 − −3	2 − −7	6 − −1	9 − −5	11 − −8
0 − −6	23 − −12	46 − −17	−2 − −3	−6 − −9
−7 − −12	−8 − −5	−15 − −6		

Negative numbers are used to express temperatures below 0 °C and money owing.

1 The temperature today in London is 12 °C. In Moscow, it is 15 degrees colder. What is the temperature in Moscow?

2 In Siberia it is 9 degrees colder than in Moscow. What is the temperature in Siberia?

3 I started with £14.30 in the bank then withdrew £25. How much do I now owe the bank?

4 I then withdrew a further £15. Now how much do I now owe the bank?

5 The lowest temperature possible is −273 °C. At the North Pole, it is 190 degrees warmer than this. What is the temperature at the North Pole?

APPROXIMATING
Calculations

Some calculations are too difficult to work out exactly in your head. But you can get an approximate answer by changing the numbers into ones you can calculate with more easily:
e.g. $18 \div 4.9$ is approximately $20 \div 5 = 4$

Work out these in your head.

$31 \div 4.7$	$52 \div 9.8$	$98 \div 19.75$
3.2×6.85	17.7×5.4	11×296
$97.6 \div 1.8$	$4.6 \div 9.9$	$18.3 \div 19.1$
48×3.25	0.92×103	96×505
$21 \times 9.5 \div 3.7$	$82 \div 19 \times 28$	$310 \div 46 \times 1.8$
$6.2 \times 89 \div 276$		

Your answers do not have to agree with those given here. They just need to be close.

APPROXIMATING **Percentages**

TOP*tips*

- **50% of something** is the same as $\frac{1}{2}$ **of it**.

- **25% of something** is the same as $\frac{1}{4}$ **of it** (so **divide** by **4**)

- **75 % of something** is the same as $\frac{3}{4}$ of it (**divide** by **4** and **multiply** by **3**)

- **33% of something** is roughly the same as $\frac{1}{3}$ **of it** (so **divide** by **3**)

You can use these facts to approximate more awkward percentages.

Also, remember to change the numbers into ones you can calculate with more easily:
e.g. 47% of £4.90 Work out **50%** of **£5.00** which is £2.50.
So, the approximate answer is around **£2.50**.

Work out these in your head.

		(approximate)
49% of £7.90	52% of £9.75	£4, £5
26% of £15.99	47% of 210 people	£4, 100 people
79% of 210 people	33% of £59	150 people, £20
28% of 77 kg	91% of 1120 km	20 kg, 1000 km
9% of 42 cm	61% of £79.99	4 cm, £50
4% of 2367 cars		100 cars

SECTION B

EQUIVALENT Fractions

$\frac{3}{4} = \frac{6}{8}$ **Six eighths** is the same as **three quarters** since both the top and bottom numbers of three quarters have been **multiplied by two**.

$\frac{3}{4} = \frac{6}{8} = \frac{30}{40} = \frac{90}{120} = \dots$ **All these fractions are equivalent because each fraction represents the same part of a whole, and is obtained by multiplying both the top and bottom numbers of $\frac{3}{4}$ by the same number.**

$\frac{35}{50} = \frac{7}{10}$ Thirty-five fiftieths, in its **simplest terms**, is seven tenths, obtained by **dividing both its top and bottom numbers by five**.

So, a fraction is also **equivalent** if you **can divide** both its top and bottom numbers by the **same number**. When you **cannot divide** both the numbers any more, the fraction has been **reduced** to its **simplest terms**.

How many quarters in one and a quarter?
$1\frac{1}{4} = \frac{5}{4}$ The answer is **five**.
There are **four quarters** in **one**, plus the **extra quarter** make **five**.

Work out these in your head.

1	How many quarters in a whole?	**1**	4
2	How many quarters in a half?	**2**	2
3	How many eighths in a half?	**3**	4
4	How many quarters in one and a half?	**4**	6
5	One quarter is the same as how many eighths?	**5**	2
6	One quarter is the same as how many sixteenths?	**6**	4
7	One eighth is equivalent to how many sixteenths?	**7**	2
8	Reduce eight sixteenths to a fraction in its simplest terms.	**8**	$\frac{1}{2}$
9	Reduce four sixths to a fraction in its simplest terms.	**9**	$\frac{2}{3}$
10	Three eighths is the same as how many sixteenths?	**10**	6
11	Two thirds is equivalent to how many sixths?	**11**	4
12	Reduce six tenths to a fraction in its simplest terms.	**12**	$\frac{3}{5}$
13	Four fifths is equivalent to how many tenths?	**13**	$\frac{8}{10}$
14	Reduce fifteen twentieths to a fraction in its simplest terms.	**14**	$\frac{3}{4}$
15	How many tenths in one and a half?	**15**	15
16	How many eighths in two and a half?	**16**	20

17 Five sevenths is equivalent to how many twenty-eighths?

18 Reduce twenty-five thirtieths to a fraction in its simplest terms.

19 Five quarters is equivalent to how many eighths?

20 How many quarters in five and a half?

FRACTIONS OF AN Amount

To calculate $\frac{1}{4}$ of something, simply **divide** it by **4**:

e.g. $\frac{1}{4}$ of 12 cm is 3 cm, since $12 \div 4 = 3$

$\frac{1}{5}$ of 35 kg is 7 kg, since $35 \div 5 = 7$

TOP*tips*

Always **divide** by the bottom number (**denominator**) of a fraction.

Work out these in your head.

$\frac{1}{4}$ of 8 cm	$\frac{1}{2}$ of 20 kg	2 cm, 10 kg
$\frac{1}{4}$ of 32 m	$\frac{1}{4}$ of 48 ml	8 m, 12 ml
$\frac{1}{5}$ of £15	$\frac{1}{5}$ of 20 g	£3, 4 g
$\frac{1}{3}$ of 6p	$\frac{1}{3}$ of 21 cm	2p, 7 cm
$\frac{1}{6}$ of 30°	$\frac{1}{8}$ of 48 ℓ	5°, 6 ℓ
$\frac{1}{10}$ of 40 min	$\frac{1}{10}$ of £25	4 min, £2.50
$\frac{1}{9}$ of 36 km	$\frac{1}{12}$ of 60 mg	4 km, 5 mg
$\frac{1}{8}$ of 72p	$\frac{1}{8}$ of 20 tonne	9p, 2.5 tonne
$\frac{1}{20}$ of £150	$\frac{1}{50}$ of 4 m	£7.50, 8 cm
$\frac{1}{16}$ of 80 ℓ	$\frac{1}{100}$ of 7 kg	5 ℓ, 70 g

If $\frac{1}{5}$ of 35 kg is 7 kg, then $\frac{2}{5}$ of 35 kg must be 14 kg.

Always **divide** by the **denominator**, and **multiply** by the **numerator** (top number) of a fraction:

e.g. $\frac{3}{4}$ of 24 m is 18 m, since $24 \div 4 \times 3 = 18$

$\frac{2}{7}$ of £14 is £4, since $14 \div 7 \times 2 = 4$

Work out these in your head.

$\frac{3}{4}$ of 8 cm	$\frac{3}{4}$ of 16 years	6 cm, 12 years
$\frac{2}{3}$ of 30 kg	$\frac{2}{3}$ of 90°	20 kg, 60°
$\frac{3}{4}$ of 20p	$\frac{2}{3}$ of 18 m	15p, 12 m
$\frac{2}{5}$ of 50 mg	$\frac{3}{5}$ of £50	20 mg, £30
$\frac{3}{5}$ of 25 km	$\frac{4}{5}$ of 10 hours	15 km, 8 hours
$\frac{7}{10}$ of 20 mm	$\frac{3}{10}$ of 70 ℓ	14 mm, 21 ℓ
$\frac{9}{10}$ of £80	$\frac{5}{6}$ of 42 cm	£72, 35 cm
$\frac{2}{15}$ of 60°	$\frac{4}{11}$ of 99 years	8°, 36 years
$\frac{2}{3}$ of 1 hour	$\frac{3}{10}$ of 5 g	40 min, 1.5 g
$\frac{3}{4}$ of 1 kg	$\frac{2}{5}$ of 1 cm	750 g, 4 mm

MORE Fractions

You should also be able to work backwards from an answer:
e.g. One third of a number is 6. What is the number?
You have to **multiply** by 3 to **get back** to the number, which is 18. Check that $\frac{1}{3}$ of 18 does equal 6.

What is the number if ...

A quarter of the number is 3?	12
A half of the number is 14?	28
A quarter of the number is 9?	36
A half of the number is 70?	140
A third of the number is 5?	15
A third of the number is 12?	36
An eighth of the number is 2?	16
An eighth of the number is 7?	56
A tenth of the number is 10?	100
A tenth of the number is 4.5?	45
A half of the number is 1.25?	2.5
A quarter of the number is 1.5?	6

If two thirds of a number is 6, **divide** by 2 and **multiply** by 3 to **get back** to the number, which is 9. Check that $\frac{2}{3}$ of 9 does equal 6.

What is the number if ...
Two thirds of the number is 12?
Two thirds of the number is 10?
Two thirds of the number is 30?
Three quarters of the number is 6?
Three quarters of the number is 12?
Three quarters of the number is 75?
Three quarters of the number is 300?
Four fifths of the number is 40?
Four fifths of the number is 16?
Three fifths of the number is 24?

18
15
45
8
16
100
400
50
20
40

Percentages

Per cent means **out of a hundred** and is represented by the symbol %:

e.g. 30 out of 50 is the same as 60 out of 100 since **both numbers** have been **doubled**. So 30 out of 50 is the same as 60 per cent or 60%.

What percentages are these?

10 out of 50	40 out of 50	25 out of 50
20 out of 50	35 out of 50	14 out of 50
49 out of 50	10.5 out of 50	

20%, 80%, 50%
40%, 70%, 28%
98%, 21%

15 out of 25 is the same as 60 out of 100 (or 60%) since **both numbers** have been **multiplied by 4**.

What percentages are these?

10 out of 25	20 out of 25	5 out of 25
6 out of 25	22 out of 25	25 out of 25
9 out of 25	21 out of 25	

40%, 80%, 20%
24%, 88%, 100%
36%, 84%

3 out of 10 is the same as 30 out of 100 (or 30%) since **both numbers** have been **multiplied by 10**.

7 out of 20 is the same as 35 out of 100 (or 35%) since **both numbers** have been **multiplied by 5**.

What percentages are these?

5 out of 10	7 out of 10	2 out of 10
8.5 out of 10	5 out of 20	8 out of 20
11 out of 20	15 out of 20	39 out of 50
4 out of 25	6.9 out of 10	18 out of 20
4 out of 5	2.5 out of 5	1.5 out of 2
0 out of 30		

Answers

50%, 70%, 20%
85%, 25%, 40%
55%, 75%, 78%
16%, 69%, 90%
80%, 50%, 75%
0%

7 out of 20 can also be written as $\frac{7}{20}$ or seven twentieths. Above we worked this out to be 35% (both numbers multiplied by 5). So **seven twentieths** is the same as **35%** (thirty five per cent).

What percentages are these?

Three tenths ($\frac{3}{10}$)	Nine tenths ($\frac{9}{10}$)	30%, 90%
Four fifths ($\frac{4}{5}$)	One fifth ($\frac{1}{5}$)	80%, 20%
Six twentieths ($\frac{6}{20}$)	Eleven twentieths ($\frac{11}{20}$)	30%, 55%
One quarter ($\frac{1}{4}$)	Three quarters ($\frac{3}{4}$)	25%, 75%
Two fifths ($\frac{2}{5}$)	Four fiftieths ($\frac{4}{50}$)	40%, 8%
Three fifths ($\frac{3}{5}$)	Thirty-seven fiftieths ($\frac{37}{50}$)	60%, 74%

USING Percentages

'50 per cent of the audience were wearing black shoes.'

This means that **50** out of **every 100** people were wearing black shoes. If there were **600** people in the audience, then **300** of them must have been wearing black shoes. 50% is the same as $\frac{1}{2}$.

Work out these in your head.

50% of 400 people	200 people
50% of 300 people	150 people
50% of 30 people	15 people
50% of 60 cm	30 cm
50% of 8 hours	4 hours
50% of £19	£9.50

To work out **25 per cent** of an amount, **halve it** and **halve it again**. This is the same as **dividing by 4** or finding $\frac{1}{4}$ of the amount:
e.g. 25% of 12 cm is 3 cm, since $12 \div 4 = 3$

Work out these in your head.
25% of 400 people
25% of 100 people
25% of 20 people
25% of 16 kg
25% of 44 m
25% of 240 ml
25% of £0.80
25% of 14 seconds

To work out **75%** of an amount, first find 25% (**by dividing by 4**) and then **multiply by 3**. This is the same as finding $\frac{3}{4}$ of the amount:
e.g. 75% of 12 cm is 9 cm, since $12 \div 4 \times 3 = 9$.

Work out these in your head.
75% of 400 people
75% of 100 people
75% of 80 people
75% of 20 cars
75% of 24 hours
75% of 360 degrees
75% of £600
75% of 1 minute

300 people
75 people
60 people
15 cars
18 hours
270 degrees
£450
45 seconds

MORE Percentages

To work out **10% of something**, simply **divide it by 10**:
e.g. 10% of 70 kg is 7 kg, since $70 \div 10 = 7$

Work out these in your head.
10% of 80 kg
10% of 20 lorries
10% of 900 km
10% of 45 minutes
10% of 6 litres
10% of £0.75

8 kg
2 lorries
90 km
4.5 minutes
0.6 litres
7.5p

To work out **20%, 30%, 40%** ... of something, first find **10%** as before (by **dividing by 10**) and then **multiply by 2, 3, 4** ...

e.g. 10% of 70 kg is 7 kg   20% of 70 kg is 14 kg
    30% of 70 kg is 21 kg   40% of 70 kg is 28 kg

Work out these in your head.

10% of 40 kg	4 kg
20% of 40 kg	8 kg
30% of 40 kg	12 kg
70% of 40 kg	28 kg
10% of 150 cars	15 cars
30% of 150 cars	45 cars
60% of £30	£18
40% of 40p	16p
70% of 120 bicycles	84 bicycles
90% of 40 goals	36 goals
10% of 9 cm	0.9 cm
80% of 9 cm	7.2 cm

To work out **5%** of something, first find **10%** as before (by **dividing by 10**) and then **halve** your answer (**divide it by 2**). You are, in effect, **dividing by 20**:

e.g. 5% of £60 is £3 since $60 \div 10 \div 2 = 3$ (or $60 \div 20 = 3$)

Work out these in your head.

5% of 60 people	3 people
5% of 80 radios	4 radios
5% of 200 days	10 days
5% of 500 animals	25 animals
15% of 200 days	30 days
15% of 60 people	9 people

Money

Calculating with money is an important skill to master.

Work out the change from £5 when you spend...

£2.60	£3.20	£2.40, £1.80,
£4.08	£1.90	92p, £3.10,
£2.75	£3.05	£2.25, £1.95,
£4.63	£2.99	37p, £2.01,
£0.84	£1.27	£4.16, £3.73

In the following questions, you will have to multiply as well as subtract.

Calculate the change from £10.00 when paying for...

Answers

4 cans of drink costing £0.50 each.	£8.00
3 pairs of socks priced at £2.00 a pair.	£4.00
10 chocolate bars costing £0.40 each.	£6.00
8 balloons priced at £0.60 each.	£5.20
3 magazines costing £3.25 each.	£0.25
2 boxes of cereal costing £2.99 a box.	£4.02

In some of the following questions, it is best to round off the prices before dividing.

You have £20. How many of the following items can you afford?

Loaves of bread costing £0.50 a loaf	40
Books priced at £4.99 each	4
Towels costing £5.99 each	3
Sunglasses priced at £7.25 a pair	2 pairs
Washing powder costing £3.50 a box	5 boxes
Floppy discs priced at £0.25 each	80

To work out the cost of 7 boxes of eggs priced at 99p for each box:

$7 \times £1 = £7$ **take away** $7 \times 1p = 7p$
The answer is £6.93

Calculate the exact cost of...

5 magazines priced at £1.99 each	£9.95
3 T-shirts costing £4.99 each	£14.97
8 mugs priced at £3.99 each	£31.92
6 chairs priced at £19.99 each	£119.94
4 CDs costing £13.99 each	£55.96
3 books each priced at £7.49	£22.47

Time

You have to be careful when calculating time, since the number system for time is based on 60 and not 10:

e.g. Add 1 h and 30 min to 07:40

Adding the hour gives **08:40** and then the **30 min** gives **08:70**, but clearly this is **wrong**. **70 min** is **1 h** and **10 min**, so the answer should be **09:10**.

TOP*tips*

When adding **55 min** to a time, it is easier to **add an hour, then subtract 5 min**.

For each of the following, add on the extra amount of time to get the new time.

06:20 1 h 30 min	07:15 1 h 20 min	07:50, 08:35	
07:30 55 min	08:10 3 h 55 min	08:25, 12:05	
08:40 1 h 30 min	09:50 2 h 30 min	10:10, 12:20	
10:15 3 h 45 min	11:55 1 h 10 min	14:00, 13:05	
13:25 40 min	14:45 40 min	14:05, 15:25	
14:50 35 min	15:55 35 min	15:25, 16:30	
15:45 50 min	17:17 3 h 50 min	16:35, 21:07	
17:39 35 min	18:41 2 h 45 min	18:14, 21:26	
19:12 3 h 50 min	19:45 3 h 35 min	23:02, 23:20	
20:25 4 h 40 min	22:25 7 h 48 min	01:05, 06:13	

When working out the amount of time between 8:15 am and 10:05 am, it is much easier first to **add 2 hours** on to 8:15 am, which gives **10:15 am**. Then **take away 10 minutes** to get 10:05 am. The answer is **2 hours take away 10 minutes** which is **1 h 50 min**.

How many hours and minutes between these times?

6:15 am and 7:45 am		1 h 30 min
7:50 am and 8:10 am	8:55 am and 9:30 am	20 min, 35 min
9:25 am and 11:50 am		2 h 25 min
10:45 am and 11:38 pm	11:24 am and noon	53 min, 36 min
11:15 am and 1:30 pm		2 h 15 min
11:50 am and 2:35 pm		2 h 45 min
12:10 pm and 4:04 pm		3 h 54 min
12:25 pm and 3:05 pm		2 h 40 min
12:51 pm and 6:17 pm		5 h 26 min
3:48 pm and 9:34 pm		5 h 46 min
10:07 pm and midnight		1 h 53 min
10:32 pm and 2:15 am		3 h 43 min
11:13 pm and 4:01 am		4 h 48 min

Algebra

Letters are used to represent numbers in **expressions**, **formulae** and **equations**.

You need to practise replacing the letters by numbers and working out the **value** of expressions:

e.g. If y is 7 then $\quad 2y$ is 14 $\quad y + 4$ is 11

$\qquad\qquad\qquad 3y - 2$ is 19 $\quad \frac{y+3}{5}$ is 2

TOP*tips*

Remember that $2y$ means 2 **times** y and $\frac{6}{y}$ means 6 **divided** by y.

If h is 6, work out the value of these expressions.

$2h$	$h + 3$	$h - 5$	$3h + 1$
$4h - 4$	$\frac{h}{2}$	$\frac{h}{3} + 4$	$\frac{h+4}{5}$

12, 9, 1, 19

20, 3, 6, 2

Sometimes, an expression is written as one letter equalling another letter. The two letters are said to form an **equation** or **formula**. If you know the value of one letter, you can work out the corresponding value of the other letter:

e.g. If $w = 3d - 2$, you can work out w for different values of d. When d is **5**, w is **3 times 5 take away 2**, which is 13. The **value** of w is **13**.

Work out the value of w when d is 6 in these formulae.

$w = d - 2$	$w = 4 + d$	$w = 3d$
$w = 10 - d$	$w = \frac{d}{3}$	$w = 2d + 3$
$w = 4d - 5$	$w = \frac{d}{2} - 1$	$w = \frac{d+10}{4}$
$2w = 3d$	$w = d^2$	$4w = 5d - 2$

4, 10, 18

4, 2, 15

19, 2, 4

9, 36, 7

You should also be able to **solve equations** which contain just one letter. To solve an equation, you work out the value of the letter which makes the equation correct:

e.g. Solve $9 - x = 4$

The answer to this is $x = 5$ since $9 - 5$ is 4

Solve each of these equations for *x*.

$x + 3 = 5$	$x - 2 = 7$	$10 = x + 4$	
$8 - x = 7$	$2x = 14$	$25 = 5x$	
$\frac{x}{2} = 5$	$\frac{x}{3} = 4$	$\frac{x}{5} = 1$	
$2x + 3 = 7$	$2x - 1 = 5$	$3x + 1 = 10$	
$11 - 4x = 3$	$\frac{x+1}{2} = 4$	$\frac{x-2}{3} = 2$	
$3(x + 1) = 6$	$2(x - 3) = 8$	$x^2 = 9$	$\sqrt{x} = 4$

Angle

Remember:
A **right-angle** is **90°**.

The two **angles on a straight line** always add up to **180°**.

e.g. If one of the angles is 45°, the other must be 135°:
    45° + 135° = 180°.

Two angles fit together to make a straight line. One of the angles is given. Work out the other one.

100°	60°	90°	65°
125°	95°	15°	4°
108°	37°	116°	89°

The **three internal angles** of a **triangle** always add up to **180°**.

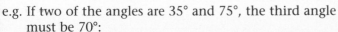

e.g. If two of the angles are 35° and 75°, the third angle must be 70°:
    35° + 75° = 110° and then 180° – 110° = 70°.

Two of the angles in a triangle are given. Work out the size of the third angle.

60°, 60°	80°, 80°
75°, 75°	10°, 30°
60°, 90°	45°, 90°
35°, 65°	55°, 70°
115°, 35°	75°, 45°
48°, 32°	16°, 54°
54°, 44°	83°, 35°
116°, 28°	37°, 49°

Area AND Perimeter

The **area of a triangle** is given by **Base × Height ÷ 2**:
e.g. The area of the triangle
shown is 33 cm².
11 × 6 = 66 then halve 66,
which gives 33 cm².

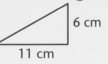
6 cm
11 cm

Notice that you could also halve the 6 first and then multiply by 11.

The base and height of 16 triangles are given below. Work out the area of each triangle.

5 cm, 4 cm	6 cm, 6 cm
7 cm, 4 cm	2 cm, 15 cm
8 cm, 7 cm	14 cm, 3 cm
3 cm, 3 cm	5 cm, 5 cm
1 cm, 11 cm	8 cm, 12 cm
7 cm, 20 cm	5 cm, 18 cm
12 cm, 12 cm	6 cm, 13 cm
9 cm, 7 cm	7 cm, 11 cm

When you know the perimeter of a square, you can work out its area by first finding the length of each side.
e.g. The perimeter of a square is 12 cm.
To get the length of each side **divide by 4** (since all the sides are equal). This gives 3 cm, so the area of the square is **3 × 3 = 9 cm²**.

3 cm
3 cm

Calculate the area of these squares whose perimeters are given in cm.

8	20	4	32
16	36	2	4t

You can find the perimeter of a square from its area by reversing the process:

e.g. The area of a square is $36\,cm^2$. To find the length of its sides, you must find which number **multiplied by itself makes 36**. This is also called **finding the square root**. The number is **6**. Since this is the length of each side, the perimeter is **6 × 4 = 24 cm**.

Calculate the perimeter of these squares, whose areas are given in cm^2.

9	25	4	100
16	144	s^2	$4s^2$

A rectangle is 3 cm wide. If its length is twice its width, calculate its area.

A rectangle's length is 4 m greater than its width. If its area is $21\,m^2$, calculate its perimeter.

Volume

The volume of a cuboid is given by
height × width × length.
e.g. The volume of the cuboid shown is
$$6 \times 1 \times 2 = 12 \text{ cm}^3$$

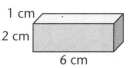

1 cm
2 cm
6 cm

Find the volume of each of these cuboids:

1 cm, 5 cm, 4 cm	4 cm, 3 cm, 2 cm
2 cm, 2 cm, 7 cm	3 m, 5 m, 2 m
4 cm, 3 cm, 3 cm	8 mm, 3 mm, 2 mm
5 m, 5 m, 4 m	10 cm, 4 cm, 3 cm
10 m, 10 m, 8.5 m	4 cm, 7.5 cm, 2 cm
5 mm, 2 cm, 2 cm	1 mm, 6 cm, 3 cm

Answers

(cm^2)
4, 25, 1, 64
16, 81, $\frac{1}{4}$, t^2

(cm)
12, 20, 8, 40
16, 48, $4s$, $8s$

$18\,cm^2$

$20\,m$

$20\,cm^3$, $24\,cm^3$
$28\,cm^3$, $30\,m^3$
$36\,cm^3$, $48\,mm^3$
$100\,m^3$, $120\,cm^3$
$850\,m^3$, $60\,cm^3$
$2\,cm^3$, $1.8\,cm^3$

Measurements

The **metric system** uses units based on 10, 100 and 1000, so it is easy to learn.

Length
1 metre (m) = 1000 millimetres (mm)
1 metre (m) = 100 centimetres (cm) (so 10 mm = 1 cm)
1 kilometre (km) = 1000 metres (m)

Weight
1 gram (g) = 1000 milligrams (mg)
1 kilogram (kg) = 1000 grams (g)
1 tonne (t) = 1000 kilograms (kg)

Capacity
1 litre (l) = 1000 millilitres (ml)
1 litre (l) = 100 centilitres (cl) (so 10 ml = 1 cl)

Notice that the weight units go up by a factor of 1000.

You also still need to be able to convert from **British Imperial system** to the metric system. Learn the following conversions.

	Imperial	Metric
Length		
	1 inch	2.5 cm
	12 inches = 1 foot	30 cm
	3 feet = 1 yard	90 cm
	1760 yards = 1 mile	1.6 km
	5 miles	8 km
Weight		
	16 ounces = 1 pound	450 g
	2.2 pounds (lb)	1 kg
	1 ton	1 tonne
Capacity		
	1 pint	570 ml
	8 pints = 1 gallon	4.5 litres

Length

The tricky bit is deciding whether to divide or multiply when converting from one unit to another:

e.g. Convert 5 metres into centimetres.

There are 100 cm in 1 m, so 100 × 5 = 500 cm.

Check that this is sensible.

Convert the following into centimetres.

4 m	7 m	10 m
6.5 m	0.5 m	0.3 m
40 mm	7 mm	

400, 700, 1000
650, 50, 30
4, 0.7

Convert the following into millimetres.

3 m	6 m	2.5 m
0.5 m	4 cm	15 cm
3.5 cm	0.2 cm	

3000, 6000, 2500
500, 40, 150
35, 2

Convert the following into metres.

2 km	7 km	3.5 km
0.4 km	400 cm	150 cm
50 cm	35 cm	

2000, 7000, 3500
400, 4, 1.5
0.5, 0.35

Weight

Convert the following into milligrams.

2 g	6 g	0.5 g	2.4 g

2000, 6000, 500, 2400

Convert the following into grams.

3 kg	7 kg	0.25 kg
4.6 kg	5000 mg	500 mg
750 mg	100 mg	

3000, 7000, 250
4600, 5, 0.5
0.75, 0.1

Capacity

Convert the following into centilitres.

5 ℓ	8 ℓ	7.5 ℓ	0.4 ℓ
0.25 ℓ	3.6 ℓ	50 ml	6 ml

500, 800, 750, 40
25, 360, 5, 0.6

Convert the following into millilitres.

2 ℓ	7 ℓ	0.5 ℓ
0.75 ℓ	0.1 ℓ	60 cl
45 cl	8 cl	

2000, 7000, 500
750, 100, 600
450, 80

Probability

The probability of **something happening** is expressed as a number **between 0 and 1**. Probabilities can also be written as fractions, decimals or percentages:

e.g. The probability of picking a red sweet from a bag containing 3 red sweets and 1 yellow sweet is $\frac{3}{4}$, since there are **three red** sweets out of a **total of four** sweets. Remember that you can write $\frac{3}{4}$ as the decimal 0.75.

A fair dice is thrown once, what is the probability of throwing:

A four?　　A six?　　An even number?
A number bigger than 4?　　Anything except 2?

A pencil case contains 4 black pens, 3 blue pens, 2 red pens and 2 pencils. You choose something without looking.

What is the probability of choosing:

A black pen?　　　A pencil?
A blue or red pen?　　Not a blue pen?

Look at the spinner.

What is the probability of the spinner landing in:

Section A?　　Section B?　　Section C?

To work out the probability of something **not happening**, first find the probability that it happens, then take that number away from 1:

e.g. The probability that it will rain tomorrow is 0.85, so the probability that it won't rain tomorrow must be $1 - 0.85 = 0.15$.

1 The probability of a bus being on time is 0.7. If it is never early, what is the probability of its being late?

2 The probability of throwing a total of 10 with two dice is $\frac{3}{36}$. What is the probability of not getting a total of 10?

3 The probability that my car will start tomorrow is 0.96. What is the probability that it won't start tomorrow?

$\frac{1}{6}$, $\frac{1}{6}$, $\frac{3}{6}$
$\frac{2}{6}$, $\frac{5}{6}$

$\frac{4}{11}$, $\frac{2}{11}$
$\frac{5}{11}$, $\frac{8}{11}$

$\frac{1}{4}$, $\frac{1}{4}$, $\frac{1}{2}$

1 0.3

2 $\frac{33}{36}$

3 0.04

Averages

The **mean** of a set of values is calculated by **adding all the values together** and dividing the answer by the **total number of values in the set**:
e.g. The mean of 3, 4, 6, 7 is **5**.

Adding the numbers together makes **20. Dividing** 20 by **four** (because there are four numbers) gives you **5**.

Work out the mean of each of these sets of numbers.

1, 3, 5   2, 5, 8   3, 3, 12   7, 4, 10

6, 9, 11   2, 3, 5, 6   4, 4, 7, 9   0, 6, 10, 12

21, 23, 25 15, 60, 75   0.6, 1.5, 1.5

You should also be able to work backwards from the mean:
e.g. The mean of three numbers is 10. Two of the numbers are 7 and 15. What is the other number? If the mean of three numbers is 10, the numbers must **add** up to $3 \times 10 = 30$. The two numbers given add to make 22, so the third number must be $30 - 22 = 8$.

Each of these sets of three numbers has a mean of 8. Two of the numbers in each set are given below. Work out the third number.

5, 14, ?   10, 11, ?   5, 18, ?   0, 12, ?

This time the mean of the three numbers in each set is 15. Two of the numbers in each set are given below. Work out the third number.

15, 20, ?   13, 17, ?   6, 27, ?   11, −6, ?

Each of these sets of four numbers has a mean of 10. Three of the numbers in each set are given below. Work out the fourth number.

5, 25, 6, ?   8, 8, 8, ?   20, 3, 16, ?   15, −10, 30, ?

The mean age of two sisters is 16. If one is 6 years older than the other, how old are they?

My father is twice as old as me and our mean age is 33. How old am I?

KS3 SATs PRACTICE 1 (HIGHER)

You should ask someone to read these questions to you. Each question should be repeated once only and then you are given the limited amount of time shown for each answer. The timing starts after the question has been repeated.

5 s

1 What is fifty-four multiplied by ten?

2 How many millimetres are there in a metre?

3 Write three-quarters as a decimal number.

4 I throw two dice. The probability that I get a double is one sixth. What is the probability of not throwing a double?

10 s

5 What is three point seven multiplied by one hundred?

6 I spend three pounds twenty. How much change will I get from five pounds?

7 Fifty per cent of a number is forty-five. What is the number?

8 Two angles fit together to make a straight line. One angle is ninety-four degrees. How many degrees is the other angle?

9 How many quarters are there altogether in two and a half ?

10 Look at the formula on your answer sheet. If d equals seven, what is h?

11 Look at the cuboid on your answer sheet. Write down its volume.

12 What is eight point seven added to two point four?

13 Estimate the value of fifty-two per cent of twelve pounds ninety pence.

14 Two angles in a triangle are each seventy-five degrees. What is the size of the third angle?

15 The mean of a, b and c is ten. a is five, b is twelve. What is c?

16 Look at the calculation on your answer sheet. Work out the answer.

17 Look at the equation on your answer sheet. What is the value of y?

18 How many sixteenths are there in five eighths ?

15 s

19 What is the cost of six mugs at two pound ninety-nine pence each?

20 Look at the expression on the answer sheet. Multiply out the expression.

21 Estimate the value of four hundred and five divided by forty-nine.

22 Each side of a square is fifty-three centimetres. What is its perimeter?

23 Look at the formula on your answer sheet. If a equals eight, what is b?

24 Thirty per cent of a number is fifteen. What is the number?

25 Look at the calculation on your answer sheet. Write an approximate answer.

26 The sum of x and y is eleven. The product of x and y is twenty-eight. What are the values of x and y?

27 Multiply twenty-five by thirty-six.

28 On your answer sheet are two numbers. Write the number which is halfway between them.

29 A square has area sixty four metres squared. What is its perimeter?

30 x equals two and y equals five. Work out the value of y to the power x take away x squared.

Time: 5 seconds

1	
2	mm
3	
4	$\frac{1}{6}$

Time: 10 seconds

5	
6	£
7		50% 45
8	degrees	94°
9	
10	$h =$	$h = 6d - 12$
11	cm³	2 cm 5 cm 3 cm
12		8.7 2.4
13	£	52% £12.99
14	degrees
15	$c =$	10 $a = 5$ $b = 12$
16		$\frac{15.7}{3.6 + 6.4}$
17		$25 - 3y = 10$
18	

Time: 15 seconds

19	£	6 £2.99
20		$4x(x + 3)$
21		405 49
22	cm
23	$b =$	$b^2 = \frac{a}{2} + 12$
24		30% 15
25		$\frac{39.81 \times 3.0}{5.95}$
26	and	11 28
27		25 36
28		$2\frac{1}{9}$ 3
29	m
30		$x = 2$ $y = 5$ $y^x - x^2$

KS3 SATs PRACTICE 2 (HIGHER)

You should ask someone to read these questions to you. Each question should be repeated once only and then you are given the limited amount of time shown for each answer. The timing starts after the question has been repeated.

5 s

1. What is fifty-six divided by seven?
2. How many kilograms are there in a tonne?
3. There are five red sweets and three green sweets in a bag. I choose a sweet at random. What is the probability that I choose a green sweet?
4. A quarter of a number is two point five. What is the number?

10 s

5. Look at the calculation on your answer sheet. Work out the answer.
6. In a group of sixty-five children, twenty-eight are boys. How many are girls?
7. A film starts at half past eight. It lasts for one hour and forty minutes. At what time does the film finish?
8. Look at the measurements on your answer sheet. Which one is roughly the same as one inch? Circle your answer.
9. Fifteen per cent of a number is twenty-two. What is thirty per cent of the number?
10. What is seven point eight multiplied by one thousand?
11. Look at the equation on your answer sheet. What is the value of x?
12. Look at the triangle on your answer sheet. What is the area of this triangle?
13. The probability that it will snow in September is nought point one five. What is the probability that it will not snow in September?
14. Sam got twelve out of twenty on a test. What percentage did he get?
15. Write another fraction that is equivalent to two-fifths.
16. The mean of a, b, and c is five. a is two, b is nine. What is c?
17. Write an approximate answer to the calculation on your answer sheet.
18. Look at the expression on your answer sheet. Multiply out the expression.

15 s

19. What is seventeen multiplied by nine?
20. Look at the formula on your answer sheet. If s equals three, what is the value of t?
21. Two of the angles in a triangle are fifty-eight degrees and seventy-five degrees. How many degrees is the other angle?
22. How many twentieths are there in four fifths?
23. A square has a perimeter of eighty centimetres. What is the area of the square?
24. Forty per cent of a number is eight. What is the number?
25. Look at the formula on your answer sheet. Write an expression, in terms of h, for d plus six.
26. Look at the calculation on your answer sheet. Write an approximate answer.
27. Multiply sixty-two by ninety-eight.
28. On your answer sheet are two numbers. Write the number which is halfway between them.
29. A cube has volume sixty-four centimetres cubed. What is the length of each edge?
30. Estimate the square root of nine hundred and ten.

Time: 5 seconds

1	

2		kg

3		5 red 3 green

4	

Time: 10 seconds

5		$6 \times (5 + 4)$

6		girls

7	

8		0.25 cm 2.5 cm 25 cm 0.25 cm

9		15% 22

10	

11	$x =$	$4x + 3 = 11$

12	cm²	3 cm 6 cm

13		0.15

14	%	12 20

15		$\frac{2}{5}$

16	$c =$	5 $a = 2$ $b = 9$

17		$\frac{39.7}{0.51}$

18		$2a(a + 7)$

Time: 15 seconds

19	

20	$t =$	$2t = 3s + 5$

21	degrees	58 75

22		$\frac{4}{5}$

23	cm²

24		40% 8

25		$h + 9 = d$

26		$\frac{0.29 \times 98.1}{\sqrt{25.3}}$

27		62 98

28		$4\frac{2}{5}$ 6

29	cm

30		$\sqrt{910}$

Answers

Practice Test 1.

1 540
2 1000 mm
3 0.75
4 $\frac{5}{6}$
5 370
6 £1.80
7 90
8 86 degrees
9 10
10 30
11 30 cm^3
12 11.1
13 £6.50
14 30 degrees
15 13
16 1.57
17 5
18 10
19 £17.94
20 $4x^2 + 12x$
21 8
22 212 cm
23 4 or −4 or both
24 50
25 20
26 7 and 4
27 900
28 $2\frac{5}{9}$ or $\frac{23}{9}$
29 32 m
30 21

Practice Test 2.

1 8
2 1000 kg
3 $\frac{3}{8}$
4 10
5 54
6 37 girls
7 Ten past ten
8 2.5 cm
9 44
10 7800
11 2
12 9 cm^2
13 0.85
14 60
15 $\frac{4}{10}$ or $\frac{8}{20}$ or $\frac{20}{50}$ ...
16 4
17 80
18 $2a^2 + 14a$
19 153
20 7
21 47
22 16
23 400 cm^2
24 20
25 $h + 15$
26 6
27 6076
28 $5\frac{1}{5}$ or $\frac{26}{5}$
29 4 cm
30 30

There is 1 mark for each correct answer. Add up the marks you got out of 30.

The National Curriculum Levels awarded for these tests would roughly be:

6 marks or under	Level 4
Between 7 and 16	Level 5
Between 17 and 25	Level 6
Between 26 and 30	Level 7

Your notes

First published 1999
Reprinted 1999

Letts Educational
9-15 Aldine Street
London W12 8AW
Tel. 020 8740 2270
Fax. 020 8740 2280

Text © Robert Franks 1999

Design and production by Moondisks Ltd, Cambridge

British Library Cataloguing-in-Publication Data
A CIP record for this book is available from the British Library

ISBN 1 84085 2305

Printed and bound in Great Britain

Letts Educational is the trading name of BPP (Letts Educational) Ltd

Durham Coll

on old picture posi

George Nairn

CHARLIE PIT, SOUTH MOOR. (900)

1. Charlie Pit, South Nook, was sunk in 1845 and was originally known as Quaking House Pit. Later it became West Shield Row, and, as this postcard published by Johnston of Gateshead in their 'Monarch' series shows, The Charlie Pit. Coal production ceased during the First World War and the pit was linked to the neighbouring Louisa mine and acted as a ventilation shaft for it - hence the large waddle fan on the right.

Front cover: Trimdon Colliery pictured on a postcard published by Brittain & Wright of Stockton-on-Tees in their 'Phoenix' series. It was posted in August 1916. The colliery closed in 1968.

Inside front cover: Elemore Colliery, owned by the Hetton Coal Co., had two shafts sunk between 1825 and 1827. The pit was incorporated into the Lambton, Hetton and Joicey Collieries in 1924 and closed on 1st February 1974.

Back cover (top): The first of three shafts at Murton Colliery was sunk in 1834. This postcard, published by A. & G. Taylor of London in their 'Reality' series, was posted in January 1908. Murton was known for its distinctive headgear, a German Koeppe winder. The loaded chaldron wagons on the right bear the mark 'SH' for South Hetton. The pit closed in 1991.

Back cover (bottom): South Moor Rescue Station. The Meco-Mining Engineering Co., based in Sheffield, received enquiries for 500 rescue apparatus sets, and this part of its business was later sold to Siebe Gorman Ltd. In 1925, the company relocated to Worcester and became well-known throughout the mining industry for the Meco-Moore loaders and conveyors. Postcard published by Stephen Young of Stanley.

Introduction

County Durham was built on coal and is possibly the oldest intensive mining area in England. The Romans excavated and burned coal in the area. The Bishops of Durham were among the early landowners to gain from coal; written evidence exists within the Boldon Book of 1183. Coal seams sloped from the high Pennines to the North-east coast. To the west of the county the seams were shallow and near the surface, so many Drift Mines were set up (even found in farmyards!), and, later, open-cast mining took place. Further east, the seams became deeper, even going for several miles under the North Sea. Here were sunk Durham's big pits - Whestoe, Wearmouth, Easington, Dawdon, Horden and Blackhall collieries.

Transporting coal in the early days was effected by wagonways laid with wooden rails to carry horse-drawn wagons (chaldrons) from the pits to the rivers. In the 18th century steam power meant that water could be pumped out of mines. Stationery steam engines, gravity and inclined planes meant that rope haulage could be used to transport rail wagons to staithes for loading into keel boats for onward shipment in collier boats. Durham was fortunate to have the rivers Tyne, Wear and Tees, and later Lord Londonderry's harbour at Seaham for coal shipments. After the Industrial Revolution, more and more Durham coal and coke was required to supply the nearby steel works at Consett and Teesside, which then supplied the steel to the shipyards on the Tyne, Wear and Tees.

Beamish Open Air Museum based their main town on the year 1913, the peak year of coal production in the county, when 165,246 men and boys worked in Durham's 304 pits. At Beamish today you can see an example of a Durham Colliery and have the experience of going down Mahogany Drift Mine.

Although picture postcards were introduced in Britain in 1894, it was only in 1902 when the Post Office relaxed their rules to allow the message to be written on the same side as the address that their use really took off. The period from then until the end of the First World War really was the Golden Age of picture postcards, with millions posted daily, their use being the equivalent to email, facebook or text message in today's society. Postcards posted in the morning could be delivered the same day if posted to an address in the same town.

Picture postcards were at the height of their popularity in the 1900-18 period, during which time they were used because people did not have telephones - or access to photographs of newsworthy events or personalities of the day - to send messages to friends or relatives (" *I will be arriving tomorrow by the 1.20 train"*) or show them what was going on in the sender's neighbourhood. Local views enabled people to send pictures of streets and buildings, and an added bonus was that until 1918 postcards could be posted for one halfpenny, half the letter rate. Cards were avidly collected and housed in specially-made albums, filled with examples received from friends or postcards bought from the local shop. In this period, the North-East of England had some excellent firms who published cards - Auty of Tynemouth (one of the earliest postcard publishers in Britain), Gibson and Johnston of Gateshead, Coates of Willington, J.B. Smithson of Ferryhill, Shildon and Wensleydale, and Brittain & Wright of Stockton-on-Tees, along with many other very locally-based ones. Together they provided an amazing portfolio of photographic postcards that depicted the mining industry in Durham in the early part of the 20th century. Details of publishers are provided in the captions where known.

It may seem strange to us today that cards were published showing disasters, but these were fulfilling the role of today's TV or newspaper pictures. The Barnsley firm of Warner Gothard specialised in these, producing commemorative disaster and event postcards from Northumberland to Hampshire and Somerset, including some Durham examples - two of the Glebe Colliery explosion of February 1908, and three of the West Stanley disaster a year later.

Publishers tried to have cards on sale as soon as possible after an event for obvious reasons of sales potential and topicality.

After 1918, the popularity of postcards fell sharply, and instead of a range of cards portraying a multiplicity of images, viewcards and seaside comics formed

CAUSEY ARCH 397

2. Causey Arch is the oldest single-arch railway bridge in the world. It was completed in 1726, and at peak usage over 900 horse-drawn wagons running on wooden rails crossed the arch every day, carrying coal from the nearby colliery to the River Tyne docks. Part of the route is now used by the Tanfield Railway. This postcard was posted at Burnhopefield in July 1915, sent to Misses Gibson and Smith at Newcastle-upon-Tyne with the message: *" We shall be very pleased to see you up on Sunday & will be at station to meet the 2.30pm from* (Newcastle) *Central"*.

the bulk of postcard output. The doubling of the postage rate for cards, increased use of the telephone and more photographic content in newspapers all diminished the use of cards to show local events. Some continued to be featured on cards, but these are much harder to find.

George Nairn
December 2016

3. Cornsay Colliery, where coal was converted into coke on the spot in 270 coke ovens. The area yielded good fireclay, so there were extensive brickworks. This postcard shows a coke wagon owned by Ferens & Love of West Brancepeth.

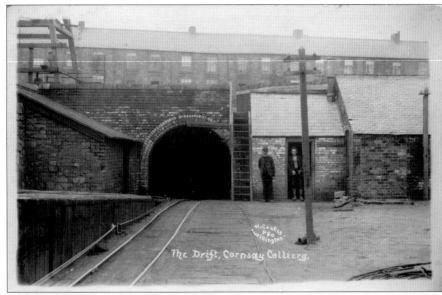

4. The Drift at Cornsay Colliery - where the drift mine goes beneath miners' houses - is seen here on a postcard published by H. Coates of Willington. The card has a Cornsay Colliery June 1913 postmark on the reverse and the message refers to the fact that there were plenty of ponies at the pit and no pit shafts.

5. Chapel Flat Drift, near Cornsay. The further west you travelled in the county, the nearer to the surface were the coal outcrops. This card, published by J.W. Rowlinson, was posted in July 1911 with the message *" we had a grand day out on Coronation Day"*. That comment refers to George V's Coronation on 22nd June.

6. Randolph Colliery, sunk in 1893, had a number of different owners over the years and a large coke works. This postcard was posted at Darlington in December 1910, sent to West Hartlepool.

7. Eldon Colliery was operated by the South Durham Coal Co. until it was taken over by Pease & Partners Ltd in 1903. It closed in 1932. The postcard was published by Brittain & Wright of Stockton-on-Tees in their 'Phoenix' series.

8. Houghton-le-Spring Colliery was opened in 1827 by Lambton Collieries, and is seen here on a card from Lilywhite of Halifax that was posted in the village in 1906. Gas works are visible on the left, and miners' houses to the right. The colliery closed in 1981.

9. Elemore Colliery was sunk in 1825 for the Hetton Coal Co. Ltd and was incorporated into Lambton & Hetton Collieries in 1896 (joined by Joicey in 1924). This real photographic postcard by unidentified publisher, posted at Sunderland on Christmas Eve 1904, shows lots of chaldron wagons from Hetton Colliery. Elemore was shut down on 1st February 1974.

10. A Johnston-published postcard of Fishburn Colliery. This overall view shows the colliery, coke works, a by-product plant and Baum washery. Due to geological problems, the colliery closed in 1973.

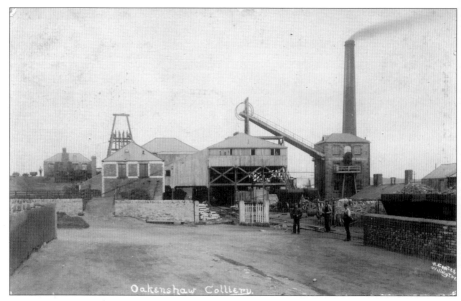

11. Oakenshaw Colliery on a card from Coates of Willington, posted from that town in September 1906. Known as the Brancepeth 'B' pit, it was sunk in 1855 by Straker & Love, and closed in 1967.

12. A rare postcard of Brancepeth Colliery showing the interior of the winding house at the old pit. Published by Coates, the card was posted to Bideford in August 1907.

13. A postcard of miners underground at Brancepeth Colliery observing two minutes' silence at 1.30pm on 28th January 1936, the day that King George V was interred at St. George's Chapel, Windsor. Photographic cards of underground scenes are extremely difficult to find.

14. Marsden (Whitburn) Colliery on a card published by Gibson of Gateshead that was posted at Whitburn in October 1912. It shows laden wagons owned by the Hartburn Coal Company. As there was no road at the time between South Shields and the colliery, an unofficial railway passenger service ran for miners, quarrymen and the public. It was nicknamed the 'Marsden Rattler'.

15. Wearmouth (also known as Monkwearmouth) Colliery on a postcard published by the London firm Photochrom c.1905. At this time the colliery was owned by the Wearmouth Coal Company and became a state-of-the-art operation in National Coal Board days, with the latest mining equipment installed to harvest the millions of tons of coal reserves under the North Sea. The colliery closed in December 1993, and the only connection to it today is a large miners' lamp outside Sunderland Football Club's ground, the Stadium of Light.

16. When this postcard was published, Silksworth Colliery was owned and operated by Lord Londonderry, but it was acquired by Lambton & Hetton Collieries in 1920. Most of its coal production was shipped out of Sunderland docks. Silksworth closed in November 1971. This card was published by J. Maughan and posted at Sunderland in August 1919.

17. Ryhope Colliery was owned by the Ryhope Coal Company. Note the large pile of wooden pit props on this postcard view from H. Bradwell. The colliery closed in November 1966.

18. A Johnston postcard of Londonderry Colliery (better known as the Vane Tempest) at Seaham. The Vane and Tempest shafts were sunk in 1923 and opened three years later. The colliery closed in June 1993 and is now a modern housing estate overlooking the North Sea. Posted at Seaham Harbour in August 1929 and sent to Wellingborough, the message reads: *" Dear Mother, you will be surprised to hear that we arrived at Seaham 10.30 on Friday night. The weather was so nice we kept thinking we would go a little farther until we thought we would finish".* Motoring, cycling or walking?

19. Most Durham coal was shipped out via the rivers Tyne, Wear and Tees. Seaham Harbour was built by Lord Londonderry to move the coal from his numerous collieries. This c.1922 postcard shows lots of colliers lined up, and Seaham Bottle Works can be seen on the skyline. In 1940 one of these colliers, SS *Giralda*, was sunk by German aircraft off South Ronaldsay with the loss of the entire crew of 23.

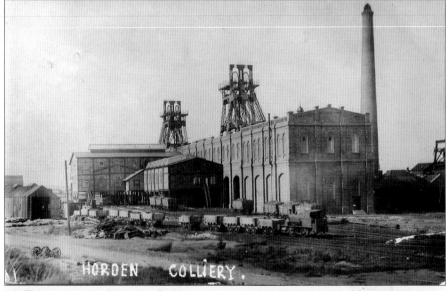

20. This postcard of Horden Colliery was posted in Hartlepool in March 1909 by an unknown photographer. It shows an 0-4-0 saddle tank engine on shunting duties. The pit closed in 1986.

21. Posted in September 1924, this Johnston-published card shows the newly-constructed Baum Washery and dry-cleaning plant at Horden Colliery, which closed in 1986.

22. Murton miners looking for coal during a stoppage. Old coal heaps and railway embankments were good sources.

Easington Colliery. 6289

23. On the right foreground in this picture of Easington Colliery can be seen evidence of one of the north-east miners' hobbies - allotments. Growing prize leeks and keeping homing pigeons were favourites. Easington, with a labour force of just over 2,700 men and boys, was one of the north-east coastal pits that stretched out under the North Sea. It closed in 1993. Another Johnston 'Monarch' series postcard.

24. " *All the men are pleased with the photo*", wrote someone on the back of this extremely rare postcard showing policemen drafted in from many areas for the Horden Colliery strike of 1910. The message continued: *"Large photos are very good and available at 2/- each. No signs of a settlement at present"*.

THEIR MAJESTIES
KING GEORGE & QUEEN ELIZABETH
VISITING A COAL MINE

25. On 29th July 1936 the then Duke and Duchess of York (the future King George VI and Queen Elizabeth) visited the Glamis pit at Kibblesworth. They went underground before visiting miners' families at their homes. The colliery was actually owned by the Duchess of York's family firm, Messrs John Bowes and Partners Ltd.

26. A Johnston postcard of Kibblesworth Colliery in the 1920s. The pit was sunk in 1935 and linked to the Robert shaft. It closed in October 1974.

Kibblesworth Colliery.

27. Tribley Pit at Hett Hills near Pelton on a rare postcard from an unidentified publisher, posted at Pelton Fell in 1913. The colliery closed a decade later.

28. Philadelphia Power Station. Lambton Collieries was amongst the first to build its own electricity generating station. Construction began in 1905, and when functioning it served not only the colliery but the engine works, colliery houses and the nearby Sunderland District Tramway system. This card was posted at Chester-le-Street in January 1908, sent to Bristol. *"Dollie was very sick & bad coming up she been laying down all day"* (sic.). Presumably the train trip didn't help!

29. Alma Colliery, Grange Villa, was sunk in 1855. This 'Monarch' series postcard shows the brickworks and colliery. It ceased production as early as 1921, and the site is now fields and woodlands.

30. A colliery locomotive working on the Lambton, Hetton and Joicey Collieries railway system. No. 550 was built in 1865 by Beyer Peacock & Co. Ltd, Manchester, and scrapped in 1954. Here it is still showing its works plate.

WILLIAM HENRY ROLLIN.

HARRY OSWALD.

JOHN DIXON.

THOMAS McNALLY.

JOHN CLARK.

THOMAS ERRINGTON.

WILLIAM GLENDINNING.

DAMAGED UP-CAST SHAFT.

GEN

14 MINERS CRUSHED AND BURNT TO DEATH, AND

CHARLES CHIVERS. PUBLISHED BY W. GOTHARD, 6, ELDON STREET, BAR

31. An explosion at Glebe Colliery, Washington, on 20th February 1908 resulted in t
a Barnsley firm, Warner Gothard, which in the 1906-14 period made a speciality of
and/or survivors. At a time when such pictures would not be available in newspap

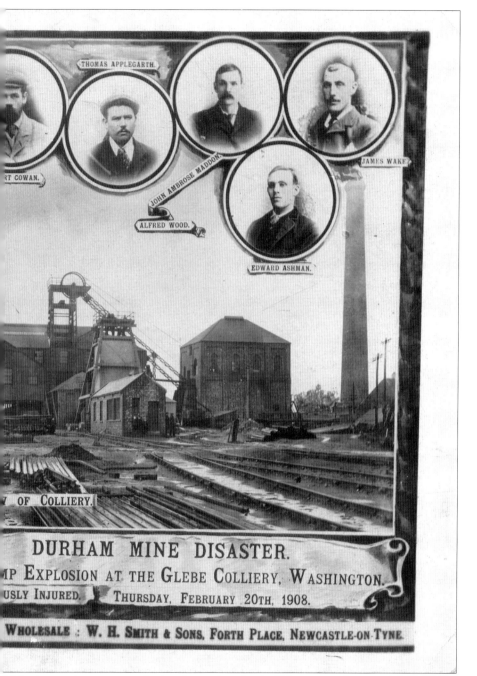

THOMAS APPLEGARTH.

JOHN AMBROSE MADDON

RT COWAN.

JAMES WAKE

ALFRED WOOD.

EDWARD ASHMAN.

OF COLLIERY.

DURHAM MINE DISASTER.

...MP EXPLOSION AT THE GLEBE COLLIERY, WASHINGTON.

...USLY INJURED. THURSDAY, FEBRUARY 20TH, 1908.

WHOLESALE : W. H. SMITH & SONS, FORTH PLACE, NEWCASTLE-ON-TYNE.

f 14 miners who were crushed or burned to death. This postcard was published by
isaster commemorative cards in this style, including vignette pictures of casualties
ds were invaluable mementoes.

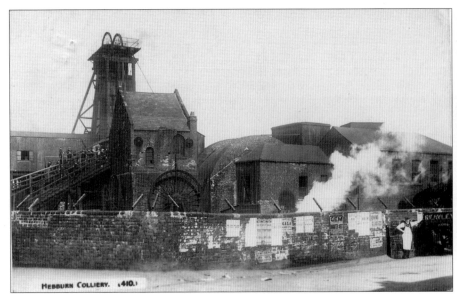

32. Hebbern Colliery on a Johnston 'Monarch' series postcard that was posted at Jarrow in February 1913 to Southsea, Hampshire. The message reads: *" The large wheel is for drawing the cage up and down for the men to descend and come up"*. Most people in Southsea in 1913 would not have seen a colliery, so picture postcards provided a useful service! Note the two spare wheels leaning against the winder house. This colliery closed in 1932.

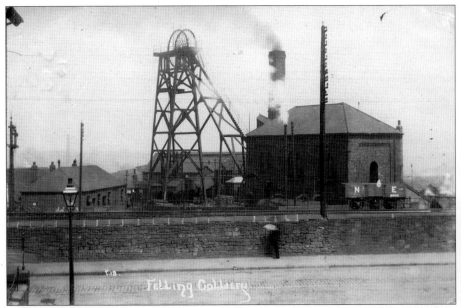

33. Felling Colliery was owned by John Bowes & partners. This postcard view was published by Gibson of Gateshead and posted from there in October 1914. The pit closed in 1931.

34. Thomas Pit, Craghead, was sunk in 1841. This Johnston-published postcard has an interesting postal history, having been sent from a British army base in France on 19th October 1915 to a Co. Down address, and approved via a red triangle censor mark.

35. In June 1920, a Black Hawthorn locomotive (South Moor no. 2) was pushing a train of wagons up the coal drops, but pushed them off the end and landed on top of them. Somehow the loco was recovered, repaired and back working again. Card in the Johnston 'Monarch' series.

Washington Disaster Funeral Feb 1908 No1.

36. Funeral of the Washington Glebe Colliery disaster victims. Around 22,000 people were present as some of the men were buried. People came from all over County Durham and Northumberland to pay a final tribute.

Scene of the Washington Pit Explosion Feb. 20th 1908.

37. In the course of the Glebe Colliery explosion, the rescuers were driven back six times. This postcard of the scene was published anonymously and posted at Newcastle in June 1908, five months after the disaster.

38. Another explosion occurred at the Burns Pit, West Stanley, on 16th February 1908, and again the disaster, where 168 men and boys lost their lives, was commemorated on a postcard published by Gothard of Barnsley.

39. A postcard produced by the Wholesale Trading Co., Newcastle, showing William Gardner and the pit pony he rescued from the 1909 disaster scene. William was one of only 30 survivors of the explosion.

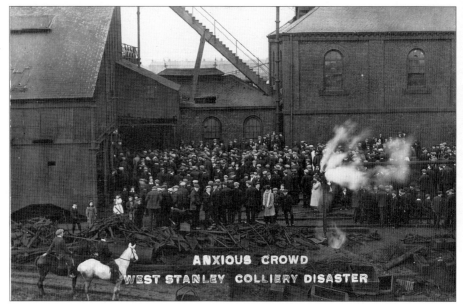

40. Thousands headed for the Burns Pit, Stanley, soon after the explosion to wait for news of loved ones. This postcard view was published by C. Smithson of Shildon.

41. The funerals of the victims of the Burns Pit disaster began on 21st February 1909, when an estimated 200,000 people came to the town on that first day. Many of the victims were buried in mass graves at St. Andrew's Church, Stanley.

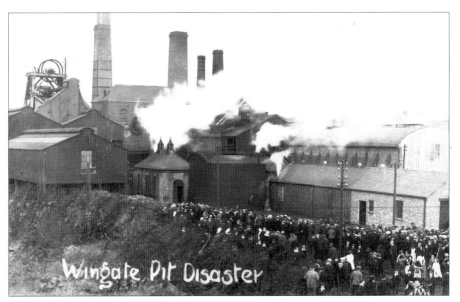

42. Another colliery tragedy took place at Wingate Grange on 14th October 1906, when an explosion, probably caused by firedamp after shot firing, ripped through the pit, killing 26 men.This postcard by unknown photographer, posted soon after the disaster, shows the crowds waiting for news.

43. Another card of an anxious crowd at Wingate, posted on 19th October 1906. The colliery closed in October 1962.

RESCUE and FIRE BRIGADE, CROOK. 2260.

44. The Miners' Rescue Station near Crook featured on a Johnston 'Monarch' series postcard, showing a Merryweather fire engine and rescue tender. The message on the reverse reads: *" Originally it was intended for fires and explosions in mines, but now it goes for fires anywhere. The firemen are very brave, and they went to the big West Hartlepool dockyard fire and did good work. Daisy"*. The fire referred to was a timber yard incident on 4th January 1922, which left 80 people homeless and could allegedly be seen as far away as Doncaster.

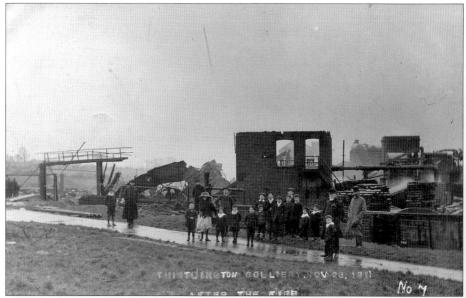

45. Thrislington Colliery on a locally-published card by Joe Gardner of Cornforth that shows the colliery after a fire on 26th November 1911. The pit closed in March 1967.

FIRE and RESCUE STATION, HOUGHTON-LE-SPRING. 1097.

46. Houghton Rescue station opened in 1913, one of several that aimed to deal with fires at collieries, both on the surface and underground, with a fire engine and rescue vehicle. Rescue workers' houses can be seen on the right of the picture. The building is still used today for firefighting, confined space industry and first aid courses. Postcard in the 'Monarch' series.

MAINSFORTH COLLIERY.

47. Mainsforth Colliery, owned in 1904 by the Carlton Iron Co. and absorbed by Dorman, Long & Co. in 1923. Note the close proximity of the workers' houses to the colliery, seen on this postcard published by J.B. Smithson of Ferryhill, sent from that town in September 1912 with the message " *I am sending you this for your album*".

NORTH FRONT CONISHEAD PRIORY CONVALESCENT HOME FOR DURHAM
MINE WORKERS. ULVERSTON.

48. Conishead Priory was opened on 23rd August 1930 as a residential holiday home for pit workers. Miners who wanted to spend a week (later extended to a fortnight) there applied to the Lodge secretary and names were chosen by ballot. Conishead provided health and recreation of mind and body for some 2,000 men each year. This postcard was posted in May 1935 at Ulverston.

49. A group of Durham miners outside the main doorway at Conishead Priory. During the Second World War it was used as a military hospital, then returned to the Durham Miners' Association until closure in December 1969. The Priory was bought by a Buddhist group in 1976 and is currently open to the public.

50. Durham miners had many pastimes, including games of quoits, football and cricket, looking after whippets and pigeons, and growing prize leeks. This proud pair are from Waldridge.

51. Waldridge miners preparing dinner for children during the 1921 miners' strike, which lasted from 1st April - 1st July.

52. A Durham Miners' Association banner depicting the old Miners' Hall in North Road, Durham, about to leave Waldridge for the Durham Gala in the early years of the 20th century. The Gala, or 'Big Meeting', originated in 1871 at Wharton Park, Durham, before moving to its present location on the Racecourse.

53. A group of miners beneath the legs of the construction of the new shafts at Easington Colliery c.1910. Easington had its own tragedy on 29th May 1951, when an explosion killed 81 miners. The three nearest rescue stations, Hougton, Crook and Elswick, all responded. Easington closed in 1993 and was demolished the following year. Postcard sent from Easington on Boxing Day 1910.

Shotton Colliery Silver Model Prize Band. June 21st 1924.

54. Shotton Colliery Band on 21st June 1924. Colliery bands were extremely popular at the time, especially on Durham Gala Day. One of the most famous was the St. Hilda Colliery Band, which won the 1,000 guineas trophy at the Crystal Palace five times between 1912 and 1926.

Aged Miners Homes. LANGLEY PARK, Opening Ceremony By Mrs Clarence D. Smith, July 5th 1924.

55. The opening ceremony of the Aged Miners' Homes at Langley Park on 5th July 1924. The association that set these up was begun in 1896 by Joseph Hopper, a miner and lay preacher. The 1920s was its peak period of building, but the project still continues from the Association's headquarters in Chester-le-Street.

56. Sacriston Shield Row Drift on a rare postcard published by an unknown photographer that was posted in Sacriston in July 1904. The Drift was worked under the hillside below the Heugh, and operated from 1900 until 1947.

57. A group of miners standing on the gantry at Sacriston Colliery with their safety lamps and sticks. The colliery closed in 1985 and seven pit ponies were found new homes. One of them, 'Pip', moved to Beamish Museum and enjoyed the rest of its days in semi-retirement, attracting lots of affection from the thousands of visitors.

58. A Johnston postcard shows the 2' 2" tramway from Chopwell towards Whittonstall. This was the first electrically-operated railway using overhead wires in Co. Durham. The loco on this postcard was built by Siemens between 1908 and 1910, and could be *Whittonstall*, scrapped in 1930.

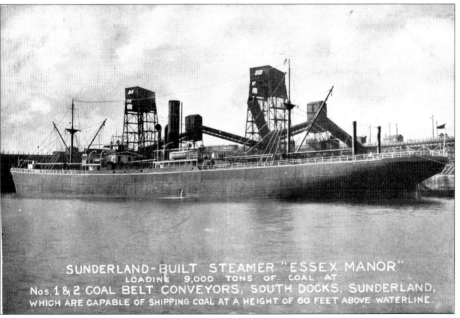

SUNDERLAND-BUILT STEAMER "ESSEX MANOR"
LOADING 9,000 TONS OF COAL AT
Nos. 1 & 2 COAL BELT CONVEYORS, SOUTH DOCKS, SUNDERLAND,
WHICH ARE CAPABLE OF SHIPPING COAL AT A HEIGHT OF 60 FEET ABOVE WATERLINE.

59. An advertising postcard for Sunderland Docks produced by the River Wear commissioners, extolling the exceptional facilities for dealing with coal cargoes, bunker coal, iron ore, grain, timber, esparto, petroleum, shipbuilding, engineering, dry docking and repairing.

60. The Harraton strike: wives and children protesting against the employment of strike-breakers are seen on this postcard being escorted by police along the waggonway at Fatfield. Harraton Colliery was known locally as 'Cotia' and closed in 1965.

61. Chester Moor Colliery was situated at the side of the main London-Newcastle railway line, with a rail link to this and to the old A1 Great North Road (now the A167). This postcard dates from c.1906 and was published by Gibson of Gateshead. The colliery closed in 1967.

62. Blackhall Colliery was owned by Horden Collieries Ltd and sinking started in 1909. It closed in 1981. This is another stuning real photographic postcard published by Johnston.

63. A postcard of Shotton Colliery published by H. Coates of Willington. The message on the card explained that there were always lots of boys bathing in the pit pond because the water was warm. No health and safety there, then!

64. Boldon Colliery was owned by The Harton Coal Co. Ltd. This Johnston 'Monarch' series card shows the North Eastern Railway track that ran from Newcastle to Sunderland. Boldon Colliery station was known as Brockley Whins until 1926. The colliery closed in 1982.

65. This is an anonymously-published postcard of Langley Park Colliery, owned by Consett Iron Co. As far back as 1873 most of its output was converted to coke in the adjacent works. The pit closed in October 1975.